MW00696200

EMBODY
YOUR
MAGICK

EMBODY YOUR YOUR MAGICK

A GUIDED JOURNAL FOR THE MODERN WITCH

GABRIELA HERSTIK

A TarcherPerigee Book

tarcherperigee
an imprint of Penguin Random House LLC
penguinrandomhouse.com

TarcherPerigee with tp colophon is a registered trademark of
Penguin Random House LLC.

Most TarcherPerigee books are available at special quantity discounts for bulk purchase
for sales promotions, premiums, fund-raising, and educational needs. Special books or
book excerpts also can be created to fit specific needs. For details, write
SpecialMarkets@penguinrandomhouse.com.

Library of Congress Cataloging-in-Publication Data

Names: Herstik, Gabriela, author.
Title: Embody your magick: a guided journal for the modern witch / by Gabriela Herstik.
Description: New York: TarcherPerigee, an imprint of Penguin Random House, 2020.
Identifiers: LCCN 2020019552 | ISBN 9780593329542 (paperback)
Subjects: LCSH: Magic. | Witchcraft.
Classification: LCC BF1611 .H53 2020 | DDC 203/.3—dc23
LC record available at https://lccn.loc.gov/2020019552

Printed in the United States of America
1 3 5 7 9 10 8 6 4 2

This book is dedicated to the Goddess

How to Work with This Journal

Welcome, witches, mystics, muses, and poets. I am so thankful you are here. This journal will lead you into embodying your magick and refining your craft, on a spiral path back into your power and all the transcendent and transformative crevices of your soul. Bring a sense of curiosity, and a yearning to meet your magick face-to-face to better weave it into your life.

This book contains magick for the physical body, the mental body, the emotional body, the spiritual body, and the soul, aiding you in finding empowerment in a holistic and personalized way. To use it, simply think of what sort of guidance you need in the moment and find the appropriate section. Or work through from beginning to end—it is completely up to you.

Through grounding rituals, breath work, tarot, spells, elemental magick, and more, you will craft your own sort of DIY alchemy. The practices that serve you best are the ones that resonate with you. Let this journal be a starting point in inviting in more magick, and conjure accordingly!

P.S. You may want to have a notebook or grimoire to accompany this journal in case you need extra space to brainstorm, contemplate, freewrite, or doodle; creativity is always encouraged!

APPENDIX 1

Elemental Correspondences

Element	Direction	Archangel	Sense	Herbs
Earth	North	Uriel/Ariel	Touch	Rosemary, frankincense, bay leaf, oak, daisy, clover
Air	East	Raphael	Smell	Lavender, eucalyptus, rosemary, dandelion, mugwort, honeysuckle, nettle, thyme, sandalwood
Fire	South	Michael	Sight	Cinnamon, basil, carnation, clove, vanilla, vervain, tobacco, cumin, devil's shoestring, cayenne, mandrake, dragonsblood, Saint-John's-wort, deer's tongue
Water	West	Gabriel	Taste	Rosemary, apple, chamomile, catnip, poppy, ginseng, rose, gardenia, jasmine, birch, watercress
Spirit	Up	Metranon		This one doesn't have as clear associations: aphrodisiacs; herbs like pomegranate, butterfly pea, rose, nettle, ashwagandha

These tables of correspondences will help you customize
your rituals and spell work. And so it is.

Crystals	Colors	Magick	Astrological signs
Black tourmaline, onyx, hematite, obsidian, all crystals since they come from the earth	Green, black, brown, gray, the colors of the earth, neutrals	Wealth, abundance, prosperity, boundaries, protection, grounding, commitment, loyalty, home	Capricorn, Taurus, Virgo
Selenite, clear quartz, smoky quartz, sodalite, celestite, fluorite, lapis lazuli, lepidolite	Yellow, white, silver, iridescent, gossamer	Business, legal problems, communication, travel, inspiration, knowledge, breath work, astral travel, divination	Aquarius, Gemini, Libra
Carnelian, citrine, orange calcite, pyrite, tiger's eye, bloodstone, garnet, ruby, peridot	Red, orange, yellow, gold	Transformation, initiation, sexuality, passion, confidence, release, adventure, banishment	Aries, Leo, Sagittarius
Amethyst, blue lace agate, jade, moonstone, pearl, topaz, malachite, rhodonite	Blue, purple, indigo, silver, white, light pink	Divination, shadow work, love, healing, self-love, karmic and ancestral healing, pleasure, intuition and psychic work, dream work	Pisces, Cancer, Scorpio
Clear quartz, labradorite, charoite, herkimer diamond, selenite	Silver, gold, the rainbow, all colors	Spiritual development, connecting to your intuition, karmic untangling, past life work, enlightenment, channeling and working with deities	

APPENDIX 2

Correspondences of Herbs

Properties	Herbs
Love	Herbs of Venus, acacia flower, jasmine, lavender, mistletoe, myrtle, valerian, vervain, violet, rose, gardenia, apple, and cinnamon
Protection	Basil, feverfew, hyssop, laurel, motherwort, nettle, juniper, yerba santa, mullein, cascarilla (powdered eggshells), patchouli, rosemary, rowan, sandalwood, frankincense, myrrh, cinnamon, and vervain
Healing	Lavender, carnation, rosemary, gardenia, garlic, ginseng, hops, mint, saffron, rowan, rue, eucalyptus, and peppermint lemon balm
Psychic work	Dragonwort, mugwort, ginseng, laurel leaves, saffron, chamomile, dandelion, skullcap, catnip, clover, mint, and nutmeg
Manifesting	Bamboo, beech, dandelion, ginseng, pomegranate, mint, rosemary, sandalwood, violet, and walnut
Creativity	Laurel, lavender, cinnamon, myrtle, valerian, and orange
Banishing/binding	Cascarilla, nettle, devil's shoestring, bamboo, benzoin, cayenne, rosemary, frankincense, mandrake, and peppermint
Wealth	Balm, High John the Conqueror root, lavender, mandrake, oak leaf, saffron, valerian, mint, cinnamon, and citrus

APPENDIX 3

Correspondences of Color

Color	Meaning
Red	Passion, sexual love, vitality, heat, health, attraction, fire
Pink	Love, femininity, nurturing, protection of children and healing, the heart, tenderness, feeling, bliss
Orange	Encouragement, creativity, stimulation, warmth, attraction, power
Yellow	Confidence, inner strength, power, vitality, vigor, self-awareness, happiness, energy, masculinity
Green	Finance, luck, wealth, prosperity, abundance, healing, heart opening, the energy of the earth, fertility
Blue	Tranquility, patience, healing, the ocean, the subconscious, dreams, femininity, relaxation
Purple	Royalty, magick, power, ambition, business progress, spirituality, connection to your third eye and higher self
Black	Absorbs negativity, darkness, night, shadow work, banishing
White	Attracts positivity, healing, light, purity, the energy of the cosmos. Cleansing and clearing as well as protective.
Silver	Celestial energy, the moon, protection, the unconscious, the heavens, the divine
Gold	Wealth, abundance, radiance, victory, money, power

EARTH:
The Physical Body

Direction: North

Archangel: Uriel

Tarot Suit: Pentacles

Zodiac Signs: Taurus, Virgo, Capricorn

Crystals: Black tourmaline, onyx, smoky quartz, all crystals because they come from the earth

Herbs: Nettle, clover, daisy, palo santo, sage, honeysuckle, jasmine, pine

Themes: Grounding, protection, boundaries, self-care, self-compassion, self-love, prosperity, abundance, wealth, shelter, home, relationships, the physical

All we have to do to remember our magick is turn our third eye to the natural world. The mother of the witches and from where all life is born, we are intrinsically connected to earth and her cycles of life, death, and rebirth. It is in our nature for we are a part of nature; human beings are creatures of Gaia, of the primordial mother. Through earth we ground, protect ourselves energetically, and work with flowers and herbs and roots. Through earth we form a foundation so that we may find abundance in all areas of our life.

In the tarot, earth is ruled by the suit of the pentacles, which teaches us of all the physical things in our lives that keep us safe and nurtured. The element speaks of our physical body, our home, our job, and what brings us financial or spiritual wealth. In this section, you will explore grounding rituals and meditations to keep your energetic body safe. You will cast spells with your clothing and use glamour as a form of self-love and self-worship. You will be guided in thinking about your body as a channel for your magick and for the mystical multitudes you contain, and you will be led in cultivating sacred self-care practices that connect you with your body in a new way.

My current relationship with earth:

very little time spent outside
a sense of disassociation

How this is a part of my magickal practice:

i try and reflect with the
moon. i neglect feeling tapped
into my body

My current relationship with grounding and nourishment:

not the best, room for
improvement, each of
nourishment

Magickal Practice: Grounding

We nourish our energetic roots through grounding—a fancy name for practices or visualizations we do to keep us firmly in this life and in this body.

What do you think of when you hear the word "grounding"?

stable, present. in - control
of my emotional responses
connected to my body
connected w/ nature + the self

Can you remember a time when you felt uprooted and scattered? What did you do to find your roots?

overwhelmed with emotion,
perhaps from february. music
helped me. well, i reconnected
with nature and my body when
i had time to take care
of myself fully. when i didn't feel
obligated.

Some ways to practice grounding include the following:

- Visualize roots growing from the base of your spine down to the crystal core of the earth. Visualize white, healing light moving up from the earth's core, through these roots and through your spine to feed your whole body.

- Place your bare feet on the earth.

- Practice a fourfold breath: inhale / hold / exhale / hold, each for four seconds. Repeat.

- Move your body! Do yoga or HIIT (high-intensity interval training) workouts, dance ecstatically, stretch, or connect with your sensuality (see page 76 for ideas).

- Stomp your feet on the ground to shock yourself into coming back into your body.

- Spend time outside, disconnected from your phone, present in the beauty and abundance of Mother Earth.

After trying a few techniques, what's my favorite way to ground?

....

....

....

....

How did this make me feel?

....

....

....

....

What are my favorite grounding rituals that weren't mentioned above?

....

....

....

....

How I ground in moments of stress or anxiety:

....

....

....

How I can ground during the day when I'm out and about (think stomping your feet, taking a deep breath, visualizing yourself melting into the earth. . . .):

....

....

....

....

Mantras

Use these mantras whenever you want to connect to the energy of the earth, to nature, to Gaia. Let these mantras guide you back into your most present and embodied state. I like to say a mantra three times; pick your favorite from the list below or write your own.

- I am grounded, protected, and divinely supported.

- I am grounded in the present moment, right here and right now.

- I am a child of the earth.

- I honor my cycles of life, death, and rebirth.

- I embrace abundance as my birthright.

- My magick supports, centers, and protects me.

- Everything I do is at the perfect time and in perfect alignment.

- I am constantly evolving, shapeshifting, and expanding my reality.

- I choose peace, I choose peace, I choose peace.

Now write your own:

- I am .... ,

.... and ....

- I am ....

- I honor ....

- I embrace .... and ....

- I connect to the element of earth through .... ,

.... and ....

- ....

- ....

- ....

- ....

Glamour Magick: Turning Your Body into a Spell

In folklore, a glamour is something that veils what lies beneath it. When we think of glamour in relationship to beauty and fashion, the esoteric meaning isn't so different—we use clothing and makeup to cultivate who we are and how the world sees us. We can turn our body into a spell by intentionally cloaking ourselves in something that makes us feel confident, protected, and centered in ourselves.

Some simple ways you can practice glamour magick:

- Wear a certain color to tap into its specific vibration and energy (see page xi).

- Dress based on an intention for the day.

- Dress based on a tarot card you pulled.

- Wear something that is inspired by the current zodiac sign of the sun or moon, or the Wheel of the Year.

- Match your outfit to the season.

- Charge your clothing with crystals on your altar.

- Wear heirloom pieces of clothing or jewelry.

- Wear garments that belong to your ancestry, religion, or culture.

- Charge an item of clothing or jewelry with an intention and turn this into a talisman. A talisman is anything you can wear or carry that holds a specific desire, which you can charge through meditation.

What piece of clothing makes me feel confident? Grounded? Capable? Sensual?

i enjoy tight clothing, high waisted + cropped, but sophisticated + artistic at the same time, huge motivable energy.

My favorite color to wear:

my favorite color, purple, black, red, pink, brown + white

How does this make me feel?

....

....

....

My favorite scent to wear:

....

....

....

How does this shift my vibe and energy?

....

....

....

My favorite tarot card and what I would wear to embody this:

....

....

....

My favorite crystal for adornment or aesthetic inspiration:

....

....

....

What talismans do I already wear? What talismans can I devise?

....

....

....

....

....

....

How do I connect with my religion, ancestry, or culture through clothing?

....

....

....

....

....

....

How can I begin this process?

....

....

....

....

....

....

Earth as the Home

In the macrocosm, the earth is humanity's home. The microcosm is our body, in which our souls and spirits reside, as well as our home, where we rest our bodies and nurture ourselves. We can work with magick to turn our home into a sanctuary.

Here's how:

- Construct an altar, the energetic focal point of a room. Set an intention (e.g., peace, healing, honoring the ancestors, working with a certain moon phase) and decorate accordingly. Think flowers, crystals, photos, talismans, and offerings.

- Cleanse with sacred smoke, using mugwort, copal, frankincense, myrrh, or ethically sourced palo santo.

- Charge a black crystal like tourmaline or onyx with the intention of protection and place it near the front entrance.

- Make a vision board (either real or digital) with your décor goals.

- Burn incense and candles, use a natural room spray or oil diffuser, or buy fresh herbs or flowers to get the mood curated and energy flowing.

- Turn cleaning into a ritual by burning incense, putting on music, wiping your counters and/or washing your floors with Florida water or rose water, and wearing something that makes you feel powerful (I love cleaning in lingerie). Cleanse with sacred smoke once you're done.

What does home mean to me?

....

....

....

....

....

How do I cultivate a sacred space in my home?

....

....

....

....

....

....

How can I make my home a temple for my spiritual practice?

....

....

....

....

....

....

What's my DREAM home? Where is it located? What does it look like?
What colors and textures would I use to decorate? What sort of
experiences would I have there?

....

....

....

....

....

....

What does it mean for me to feel safe and grounded in my home?

....

....

....

....

....

*How is my home a reflection of my inner world? What can I do to find
peace within both my home and my body?*

....

....

....

....

....

....

....

....

....

....

....

....

....

....

....

....

....

A Tarot Spread
for Honoring the Self

Taking care of yourself is a ritual of its own; it is body magick and sacred self-care. Use the following tarot spread to honestly assess what's working in your relationship with self-love and self-compassion, and what's not. You can also use an oracle deck instead of a tarot deck (for any spread in this journal).

Card 1: What is my relationship to self-care?

I pulled: ....

My interpretation: ....

....

Card 2: What self-care practices are working for me?

I pulled: ....

My interpretation: ....

....

Card 3: What self-care practices are NOT working for me?

I pulled: ....

My interpretation: ....

....

Card 4: How can I better support myself in times of turbulence, chaos, or worry?

I pulled: ....

My interpretation: ....

....

....

Card 5: How can I incorporate new self-care practices into my life?

I pulled: ....

My interpretation: ....

....

....

Card 6: How is the universe supporting me in this growth and transformation?

I pulled: ....

My interpretation: ....

....

....

Notes or insights about this reading:

....
....
....
....
....
....
....
....
....
....
....
....
....
....
....
....
....
....
....
....
....
....

Rapid-Fire Journal Questions

Answer these questions to get in touch with earth, with boundaries, with self-protection, with self-love and self-care. Don't overthink them; let the answers flow without fear or judgment. Burn some incense, make some tea, grab water, set the mood, and dive in.

What magickal practices can I work with to love my body when I'm having trouble with that?

....

....

....

....

This is a simple affirmation I can use to remember to love my body:

....

....

....

....

What glamour rituals do I have in place to remind me of my beauty, inside and out?

....

....

....

This is a glamour ritual I can incorporate into my practice to remind me of my essence and radiance:

....

....

....

This tarot card inspires me to find grounding and power in my body:

....

....

What sensory experiences do I associate with earth?

....

....

How do I establish boundaries that protect and serve me?

....

....

....

....

How do I feel when I say NO?

....

....

....

....

....

....

What practices do I have or can I cultivate to help me find strength in my boundaries?

....

....

....

....

....

....

My favorite way to connect to the earth goddess within myself:

....

....

....

....

....

....

AIR:
The Mental Body

Direction: East

Archangel: Raphael

Tarot Suit: Swords

Zodiac Signs: Gemini, Libra, Aquarius

Crystals: Selenite, clear quartz, sodalite, celestite, fluorite, lapis lazuli, lepidolite

Herbs: Eucalyptus, dandelion, spearmint, lavender, lemon verbena, mistletoe, mugwort, nutmeg, peppermint, sandalwood, thyme

Themes: Thought, intellect, communication, freedom, presence, clarity, breath, cleansing, expansion, inspiration, writing, expression, revolution

Our minds are our most powerful magickal instruments. After fire sparks an idea, it is our minds that create, scheme, and analyze. It's how we transmute the non-physical to the physical, moving the ethereal into this realm. It is the only ritual tool we need, so let's learn to work with it instead of against it.

Now, let's explore the world of air—the mental body—that rules over how we process, communicate, and concoct. Air calls for expansion, movement, and freedom. You will be guided in writing invocations for when you want to channel the neverending universal force within, and explore how to train your mind to be the most positive version of itself possible.

My relationship with air:

....

....

....

....

How this is a part of my magickal practice:

....

....

....

....

....

My relationship with breath and presence:

....

....

....

....

Magickal Practice: Breath Work

No one teaches us to breathe, and we tend to hold our breath when we are anxious or worried or tense. Try taking a full breath in a confined space like an elevator—you'll probably get a weird look!

Flip the page for breathing techniques to use when you're stressed, or just need to ground a bit. Try one for at least three minutes and then see how you feel. Start with four seconds per inhale or exhale; as you get more comfortable, you can move to five, six, or seven seconds. Play around with length and breathing in through your nose and out through your mouth and vice versa to find what feels satisfying and powerful.

My relationship to my breath:

....

....

....

....

....

....

How does my body react in moments of anxiety, tension, and uncertainty?

....

....

....

....

....

....

....

....

....

....

What am I hoping to gain by forming a relationship with my breath?

....

....

....

....

....

....

....

....

....

....

....

The belly breath

How to: Inhale through your nose . . . exhale through your mouth. Feel your belly expand with air and then contract. As you exhale, let out any instinctive sounds like growls or sighs or hisses. Don't pause between inhale and exhale.

This is good for: Releasing stuck feelings, processing emotions or tensions, or if you're feeling overwhelmed

How this felt:

....

....

....

....

....

This is what came up:

....

....

....

....

....

....

The fourfold breath

How to: Inhale . . . hold . . . exhale . . . hold. Inhale and exhale through your nose.

This is good for: Grounding; finding presence in your body; relaxing; releasing worry, fear, and tension; calming the mind

Element: Earth

How this felt:

....

....

....

....

....

....

This is what came up:

....

....

....

....

....

....

The threefold breath of water

How to: Inhale . . . exhale . . . hold. Inhale and exhale through your nose.

This is good for: Cleansing the body of toxins, for healing and centering

Element: Water

How this felt:

....

....

....

....

....

....

This is what came up:

....

....

....

....

....

....

The threefold breath of fire

How to: Inhale . . . hold . . . exhale. Inhale and exhale through your nose.

This is good for: Energizing, revitalizing, finding passion and warmth

Element: Fire

How this felt:

....

....

....

....

....

....

....

This is what came up:

....

....

....

....

....

....

Alternate-nostril breathing

How to: Exhale completely and bring your right thumb to cover your right nostril. Inhale and bring your pointer finger to cover your left nostril, remove thumb, exhale and inhale through your right nostril; repeat.

This is good for: Energetic balance, coming back to the present, clearing your body and lowering stress, and strengthening the lungs

How this felt:

....

....

....

....

....

This is what came up:

....

....

....

....

....

....

The breath of fire

How to: This is done only through the nose! Inhale deeply and then exhale quickly and forcefully, feeling your stomach contract and the inhale come automatically. Keep exhaling sharply until you can't anymore. Exhale completely and start again, feeling your navel moving toward your spine with each sharp exhale.

This is good for: Clearing and cleansing the energetic body, activating the subtle body

Element: Fire

How this felt:

....

....

....

....

This is what came up:

....

....

....

....

....

This is my favorite breath:

....
....
....
....
....
....

This is my favorite time to practice breath work:

....
....
....
....
....
....

This is how I am incorporating breath work into my ritual practice:

....
....
....
....
....
....

Crafting Your Own Words of Power and Incantations

Magick teaches us of the power of words and the intention behind them. A spell needs to be both spoken and *felt*. Have you ever noticed the word "spell" is in "spelling"? Witches know all about using vibration and energy to foment change through words and will, known as magick! Sometimes all we need for a spell to work is to remember our power and declare it out loud.

While there are plenty of charms and incantations, or sacred words of power, out there, the most effective are ones that you feel connected to, so write your own that you can say whenever you need to stand firmly in your strength. Speak them before a ritual, during your morning practice, or whenever you need the universe's support.

How do I work with words, charms, and incantations in my magickal practice?

....

....

....

What's my relationship to words and magick?

....

....

....

What superstitions, sayings, and beliefs do I have around words?

....

....

....

STEP 1: FIND YOUR INTENTION

What do I want to feel with this incantation (e.g., powerful and present):

....

....

....

What do I want to invoke or conjure (e.g., the strength of the universe standing by me):

....

....

....

STEP 2: CONJURE VISUALS AND WORDS OF POWER

What words or images come to mind (e.g., grounded, the roots of a tree, the force of a lightning bolt, the ferocity of a cobra):

....

....

....

STEP 3: PICK THE FORM

At this time and at this hour I call forth (your intention) ....

through (visuals and words of power) ....

and/or

Here and now, I stand firm as the universe supports me, with perfect

love and perfect trust, I call on (your intention and visuals and words

of power) ....

and/or

I (your name) stand in my highest power to embody (your intention)

.... *and (visuals and words of power)* ....

STEP 4: ADD THE FINAL TOUCH

I always add the following caveat to my magickal workings:

This or something better for the highest good of all involved.

and/or

For the good of all, according to free will.

STEP 5: PUTTING IT ALL TOGETHER

Finish with:

So mote it be.

or

And so it is.

or

So it shall be.

and/or

The spell is done.

Here is an example to play with:

At this time and at this hour I call forth my universal power, *through* the magick of earth, air, fire, water, and spirit, I stand in balance with all that is. *Here and now, at the present moment, I stand firmly as the universe supports me, with perfect love and perfect trust, I call on* the energy of the moon and sun. I am lightning and electricity, charging up my soul with ease. I feed my magick with my love of being. *This or something better for the highest good of all. So it is and the spell is done.*

My final incantation:

....

....

....

....

....

....

....

....

....

....

....

....

....

....

During what kind of spell or ritual can I say this incantation?

....
....
....
....
....
....
....
....
....

My favorite time to say this incantation:

....
....
....
....
....
....
....
....
....
....

Describe the highest self you're calling upon: What do they look like? Feel like? Who do they remind you of? Draw or picture this version of yourself to tap into when you need to remember your power.

Mantras

Sometimes you don't need a whole incantation; sometimes a mantra or affirmation will remind you of your power. I like to say a mantra three times. Pick your favorite from the list below or write your own.

- I am present in my body and supported in my magick.

- I am inspired, connected to the cosmos, and radiant as hell.

- I return to my breath and the present moment.

- I am embodied in my power.

- I release any anxieties, worries, tension, or fear with each exhale.

- My mind is powerful and a conduit of potent magick.

- I am grounded in my truth.

- I adore, appreciate, and honor myself as magick.

Now write your own:

- I am .... ,

  .... and ....

- I am ....

- I honor ....

- I embrace .... and ....

- I connect to the element of air through .... ,

  .... and ....

- ....

- ....

- ....

- ....

- ....

- ....

- ....

Give Yourself
a Magickal Name

Names are sacred; to know a name is to know the object's or person's power. In ritual, we are another version of our waking selves; in that liminal space, we experience things in a new way, in an altered state of consciousness. If you choose, you can conjure a new name to use in ritual and in your magickal practice.

Think of what you'd like to embody in your magickal work, and what words from the natural world you want to incorporate, like animals, crystals, flowers, colors, or planetary bodies. You may also ask the universe to bring you your name in dreams, meditation, or in your waking life.

My favorite sacred associations (e.g., crystals, Goddesses, elementals, planetary bodies . . . etc.):

....

....

....

....

....

....

Things that inspire me from the natural world:

....

....

....

....

....

....

How I want to feel when using my magickal name:

....

....

....

....

....

....

My magickal name:

....

....

....

....

....

....

....

....

....

....

....

....

....

....

....

....

....

....

....

....

Cleansing with Sacred Smoke

Using smoke from burning herbs is an age-old tradition for protection and cleansing. This is a simple ritual you can perform whenever you want to purify yourself or the space you're in. Light your herbs until they catch on fire, then carefully blow them out so they smolder. If you're using a wrapped bundle of herbs, don't forget your fire-safe bowl or shell so that the ash doesn't get everywhere.

You can also use resin by putting sand in a bowl and placing a charcoal disk on top. Light the charcoal disk and wait until it begins turning white to sprinkle resin on top of it.

Try:

Ethically sourced sage—clears the air of bacteria, spiritually safeguards, banishes negative energy

Ethically sourced palo santo—a warm and inviting scent that protects and clears unneeded energy

Mugwort—ruled by the moon, enhances psychic visions and lucid dreams, heightens clair-senses

Lavender—ruled by Mercury, facilitates tranquility, healing, and relaxation

Frankincense—ruled by the sun, connects to solar energy, aids in manifesting, cleansing a space and the astral body, consecrates ritual items

Myrrh—sacred to Aphrodite, Goddess of love, illuminates the mysteries of death and rebirth, enhances awareness of energy flow in the body and in ritual

Copal—clears a space, removes mental blocks, enhances the ability to enter trance states

My favorite herb for cleansing:

....

....

....

....

....

....

How I turn this into a ritual:

....

....

....

....

....

....

How this herb makes me feel:

....

....

....

....

....

....

What kind of energy am I inviting into my space?

....

....

....

....

....

....

My favorite moon phase for working with sacred smoke:

....

....

....

....

....

....

Gaze at the smoke for five minutes and draw what you see:

A Tarot Spread to Conjure Inspiration and Your Inner Muse

Sometimes we need a little extra help to inspire our soul and our creative work. Sometimes we need a dash of inspiration to fuel our magick, and that's totally okay! Use a tarot or oracle deck to gain fresh perspectives and embrace your inner muse. Try the following spread to tap into the numinous nature of your spirit and call on your creativity, especially when you're having artist's block or when you need magickal assistance in building something new.

Card 1: Where can I look for inspiration?

I pulled: ....

My interpretation: ....

....

....

Card 2: How can I invoke this creativity from within myself?

I pulled: ....

My interpretation: ....

....

....

Card 3: How can I conjure new perspectives, new muses, and new ideas?

I pulled: ....

My interpretation: ....

....

Card 4: What message is the universe sharing for inspiration?

I pulled: ....

My interpretation: ....

....

Card 5: How can I channel my energy to honor and hone my creativity?

I pulled: ....

My interpretation: ....

....

Card 6: What can I remember when facing creative blocks?

I pulled: ....

My interpretation: ....

....

Notes or insights about this reading:

....

....

....

....

....

....

....

....

....

....

....

....

....

....

....

....

....

....

....

....

....

....

Rapid-Fire Journal
Questions

These journal questions will help you get in touch with air, with presence, with your mind and beliefs and inspiration. Don't overthink them; let the answers flow without fear or judgment. Turn this into a ritual by burning incense, getting cozy with a cup of tea, and allowing your magick to flow from mind to paper.

What are my core beliefs? What do I believe about the world, about my magick, about myself?

....

....

....

....

Are these beliefs true? Are they positive and supportive? If not, how can I reframe them to support myself and my magick?

....

....

....

When I am in ritual and ceremony, I feel the most connected to (my higher self, God/dess, ancestors, the universe):

....

....

....

When I am inspired, and creating art or magick or something new, I feel the most connected to:

....

....

....

....

My muses and inspirations are:

....

....

....

....

Write a poem about the element of air, about its freedom and expansion and presence:

....

....

....

Pick a tarot or oracle card that exemplifies the energy of air and the mental body. Journal, doodle, free write, or compose a poem or haiku in response:

What is my self-talk like? Is it negative or positive and supportive?

....

....

....

....

This is how I will make sure to be extra-compassionate with myself:

....

....

....

....

This is what I can do to make sure I'm taking care of my mental health:

....

....

....

....

My favorite way to calm my mind and find presence is:

....

....

....

....

....

These are the practices and rituals that support me in finding peace, calm, and security:

....

....

....

....

....

....

....

....

....

....

....

....

....

....

....

....

....

....

....

....

FIRE:
The Spiritual Body

Direction: South

Archangel: Michael

Tarot Suit: Wands

Zodiac Signs: Aries, Leo, Sagittarius

Crystals: Carnelian, pyrite, citrine, yellow topaz, golden calcite, fire agate, fire opal

Herbs: Cinnamon, dragonsblood, sweet basil, myrrh, oak, Saint-John's-wort, carnation, clove, garlic, juniper, rosemary, tobacco, vanilla, vervain

Themes: Passion, action, intensity, rebirth, transmution, sexuality, anger, destruction as a form of creation, seduction, evolution

We are the most powerful, and our magick is the most potent, when we *feel it;* when our vision is clear; our third eye is set; and our body and spirit is filled with the anticipation, energy, and vibration of what we want to accomplish. It is not enough to say or think about what we want; we must embody it with passion—and know that it is already in our reality. Fire rules over the spiritual body that aligns with our divine will and experiences this as truth and reality.

Fire is the element of transformation, power, action, alchemy, and destruction. Fire requires presence and intention; it is demanding and dangerous, but it can also transmute, clear away, and fortify. It is through fire that we have a personal relationship to the eternal flame in our soul.

We can use fire to banish whatever isn't serving our highest good or evolution, to meet ourselves more fully, and to connect to our power, our sexuality, and our strength. Let's dive into candle magick, banishing work, sex magick, and tarot for a more vigorous connection to this fierce aspect of ourselves.

My relationship with fire:

....

....

....

How this is a part of my magickal practice:

....

....

....

My relationship with sexuality and power:

....

....

....

Magickal Practice: Candle Magick

One of the easiest ways to get in touch with fire, and enact our will, is through candle magick. Before you begin, set your intention and what you want your spell to accomplish; candles are a potent tool for manifesting and banishing. Use the following guide in dressing and charging your candles so that you can incorporate them into your rituals.

My intention:

....

....

....

....

What this feels like in my body:

....

....

....

....

My desired result:

....

....

....

....

....

....

STEP 1: PICK YOUR CANDLE AND COLOR

Size. If you want a candle whose effects will last more than a day, pick a three- or five-day jar candle. If you want something short and sweet, try a chime, a small votive, a taper, or even a tea light candle.

Color. Use the correspondence chart on page xi to help pick a candle appropriate for the working. White is always a good choice to attract, and black to banish.

My favorite kind of candle for spell work is:

....

....

....

....

....

The color I'm using for this spell is:

....

....

....

What this color means to me:

....

....

....

....

....

....

Crystals, herbs, food, and animals I associate with this color that I can draw on for inspiration:

....

....

....

....

STEP 2: PICK OILS AND HERBS TO DRESS THE CANDLE WITH

Using the correspondence chart on page x to pick an oil and herbs to amplify your intention. You can always use honey to attract; olive oil is a good catchall.

Oils and herbs I'm using to anoint my candle:

....

....

....

....

What these represent for my spell and intention:

....

....

....

....

....

STEP 3: CARVE THE CANDLE

Carve your candle with your name, zodiac signs (to correspond the sign of the moon and sun on the day of your working) and appropriate symbols (like a $ sign, a heart for love, or an X to banish).

What I'm writing on my candle:

....

....

....

....

Symbols and esoteric symbols I can use (think pentagrams, the ankh, stars, or money signs):

....

....

....

....

STEP 4: DRESS THE CANDLE

When dressing a candle—that is, to cover it in herbs and oils—it's important to be clear on your intention:

To manifest: Rub oil from the base of the candle up toward the wick.

To banish: Rub oil from the wick of the candle down toward the base.

If you're dressing your candle with herbs, sprinkle the herbs in this same manner (and don't use too many herbs or they might catch on fire), or around the base of the candle on a plate.

You can also use a needle or a small kebab rod to pierce the base/bottom of the candle, and then put the herbs in these holes. Use another candle to drip a bit of wax to seal them inside.

This is how I'm dressing my candle:

....

....

....

I'm dressing it with:

....

....

....

....

....

STEP 5: PERFORM THE RITUAL AND READ THE CANDLE WAX

Once you've dressed the candle, you can use it for your spell and ritual. When you're done, you can read the wax to understand how your spell will turn out and any other working you may need to perform to accomplish your intention. You can also read the leftover/excess wax by interpreting any symbols or shapes you see.

The symbols and shapes I see:

....

....

....

....

....

....

....

....

....

What they mean to me:

....

....

....

....

....

....

....

....

....

....

....

....

....

....

....

....

....

....

....

....

Draw what this looks like:

You can also interpret the spell based on where the wax accumulates. Wax pillars that form when the candle is burned all the way down may represent blockages. Above the candle represents north; to the right, east; in front, south; and to the left of the candle will be west.

Excess wax flow in the north represents material or physical issues. This spell may take a bit longer to manifest. See what else you can do in real life to help it along, and know this generally means the results will be longer lasting.

Excess wax flow in the east means to look out for some kind of new download, idea, insight, or a conversation to bring your spell to reality.

Excess wax flow in the south represents the energy of passion, intensity, and vigor. This may mean that the ritual happened too quickly and that more work, like another spell or ritual or work in the mundane life, may be required.

Excess wax flow in the west deals with spirituality and psychic messages, and how the past is affecting your working.

This is where I had excess wax flow and what I think it means:

....

....

....

....

....

....

....

....

If you used a jar candle—one that you cannot remove from its container—you can also interpret how the glass reacts. If excess wax remains on the bottom or sides of the glass, there is more material work to be done. Soot represents blockages; if you see this at the top of the jar and not at the bottom, it means these blockages have been resolved. If the soot continues toward the bottom, it indicates more work to be done.

NOTE: Never leave candles unattended!

Also, *never blow a candle out*, as this is said to blow out its magick. Use a snuffer or fan the flame out if you can't let it burn all the way down. Next time you light it, refocus on your intention. Or leave it in the sink to burn down, making sure there's nothing around it that can catch on fire.

If there is excess wax left over or you're using a jar candle, throw it out in a garbage can at a three- or four-way intersection—the modern witch's crossroads.

Any notes on my spell:

....

....

....

....

What it felt like as I was performing the working:

....

....

....

Results:

....

....

....

....

....

....

....

....

....

Reminders for next time:

....

....

....

....

....

....

....

....

....

....

Mantras

We can work with mantras to remember our passion, to nourish our inner flame, to enhance our knowledge of ourselves and our magick. Use the following to inspire you, to feel yourself, to remember your strength and purpose and unyielding vibrance and spirit.

- I embrace my power fully, unapologetically, and without shame.

- I follow my passions as a path to evolution.

- I release shame around who I am and who I want to be.

- I manifest the most grounded, evolved, and vibrant version of myself possible.

- I embrace and accept my sexuality and I support its evolution.

- I connect to the divine light of the sun and cosmos whenever I need.

- My desires pave the way to the life of my dreams.

- I claim my voice, my vision, and my desires with strength and purpose.

- I use anger as a constructive route to transformation.

- I channel my rage by transmuting it through art and magick.

Now write your own:

- I am .... ,

  .... and ....

- I am ....

- I honor ....

- I embrace .... and ....

- I connect to the element of fire through .... ,

  .... and ....

- ....

- ....

- ....

Simple Sex Magick
to Own Your Power

When we're in ritual, we raise energy through a "cone of power," which we visualize as a funnel directing our energy into the cosmos. We can use our sexual energy in a similar way. To practice sex magick, consider your intention and what you want the spell to do, whether that's to call in money or banish an ex, and then masturbate (or have sex with a partner you love and trust completely—this can get energetically messy if you're not on the same page) as you focus on that intention. As you orgasm or get as close as possible, you will send this intention into the cosmos. As you settle in the afterglow, feel this energy vibrating throughout your body, and keep vibrating this intention out to the universe.

You can also use sex magick as a way to become more comfortable with your sexuality, to test your limits and edge and to feel more confident in yourself. Use the following prompts as an invitation to explore your sexuality in a supported way.

What I think of when I hear "sex magick":

....

....

....

....

....

....

What this means to me:

....

....

....

....

....

....

My relationship with sexual energy:

....

....

....

....

....

....

To draw light and energy into your body

Why: To bring power, passion, and excitement into your life, to recharge your energetic body

How to: As you masturbate, visualize your body drawing down golden, healing light from the sun. Feel this charging up your solar plexus chakra above your belly button. Continue to pull this golden solar light into this energy center and feel it flooding your body with its invigorating and inspiring vibration.

How this felt for me:

....

....

What I liked:

....

....

....

What I didn't:

....

....

....

To embrace your sexuality and release shame

Why: Because we live in a patriarchal culture, any sexuality that is not the "norm" (aka between a cis hetero man and woman) is deemed immoral. But whether you're queer, kinky, or figuring it out, you have every right and reason to embrace and explore your sexuality.

You'll need: A black crystal such as tourmaline and a red or orange crystal such as carnelian

How to: Meditate with tourmaline, thinking of any shame or fear you have around your sexuality and what is holding you down from owning this. Breathe this into the stone. Then hold the carnelian and visualize yourself as the most confident and affirmed version of yourself possible. Think of the kind of experiences you want to have and what you want to feel. Keep this carnelian next to you, on your body or pillowcase, and masturbate as you focus on this sexually confident version of yourself. As you reach a point of climax, send this intention out to the cosmos, and then bask in the energy.

Work with these stones and this meditation whenever you want to release shame and draw in confidence.

How this felt for me:

....

....

What I'm releasing:

....

....

....

....

What I'm calling in to take its place:

....

....

....

....

....

What I liked:

....

....

....

....

What I didn't:

....

....

....

....

To manifest or banish using sigils

Why: You either want to call in something new or banish something that's no longer working for you.

How to: First, get clear on what you're doing.

I am manifesting or banishing:

....

....

....

Now cross out all the repeating letters.
Letters I'm left with:

....

Use these letters to form a symbol, layering them on top of one another. Or let the intention inspire you—the weirder and less the final product looks like recognizable letters, the better. Play around until you come up with a sigil—a magickally charged symbol—you like.

My sigil:

Now on to the magick. Focus on your intention as you start to masturbate and raise energy. As you climax, or reach as close as you can, look at your sigil, sending it your desire. As you bask in the afterglow, feel the energy and intention vibrating throughout your body.

How this felt:

....

....

....

....

....

What I liked:

....

....

....

....

....

What I didn't:

....

....

....

....

....

In what other ways can I use sex magick?

....

....

....

....

....

....

How can I incorporate sex magick into other spells and rituals?

....

....

....

....

....

....

How can I work with sex magick as a devotional practice to Goddesses, Gods, or my higher self?

....

....

....

....

....

....

If I were to dedicate a sex and self-love altar, what would I include? What colors and crystals? Would I include sex toys or lube? What would I use to represent my ideal sex life?

....

....

....

....

....

....

....

....

....

....

....

....

....

....

....

....

Now go build a sex and self-love altar in your bedroom!

A Tarot Spread
for Understanding
and Deconstructing Anger

Anger is a normal feeling, and when we transmute it into passion, it can help us accomplish our goals. In the midst of ire, it can be hard to understand it and see where it's leading, but we can use the tarot to direct it constructively.

Card 1: What my anger is trying to teach me

I pulled: ....

My interpretation: ....

....

....

Card 2: The message I am meant to take from this anger

....

I pulled: ....

My interpretation: ....

....

....

Card 3: How I can transmute this anger into action and creation

I pulled: ....

My interpretation: ....

....

....

Card 4: How to stay centered and grounded through this experience

....

I pulled: ....

My interpretation: ....

....

....

Card 5: What to take from this experience moving forward

....

I pulled: ....

My interpretation: ....

....

....

Notes or insights about this reading:

....

....

....

....

....

....

....

....

....

....

....

....

....

....

....

....

....

....

....

....

Rapid-Fire Journal Questions

Answer these questions to get in touch with fire, with your passions and pleasure and inspiration. Don't overthink them; let the answers flow without fear or judgment. Burn incense, light some candles, wear something that makes you feel sexy or embodied and get to it!

How am I being transformed by sexual energy?

....

....

What am I hoping to generate for myself?

....

....

How can I use sex magick to push against the thresholds of my mind and expand my experience of reality?

....

....

How can I expand my definition of myself, of my sexuality, of sex magick?

....

....

....

What does magick feel like in my body when I'm present, impassioned, and inspired?

....

....

....

What colors do I see?

....

....

....

What do I taste?

....

....

....

What non-sexual things turn me on and feed my soul?

....

....

....

What practices can I tap into when I want to embody the erotic power of the universe?

....
....
....
....

My favorite ways to incorporate fire into my spells and rituals are:

....
....
....
....

What does the energy of fire feel like in my body?

....
....
....
....

What are the old patterns and paradigms that fire is burning away for me? What wisdom can I find in this clearing?

....
....
....

*Where am I holding on to anger and resentment? How can I let go, or work
constructively with it, to make room for feelings like passion and pleasure?*

....

....

....

....

What does pleasure mean to me?

....

....

....

....

What brings me pleasure? How can I incorporate this into my life?

....

....

....

....

....

....

....

WATER:
The Emotional Body

Direction: West

Archangel: Gabriel

Tarot Suit: Cups

Zodiac Signs: Cancer, Scorpio, Pisces

Crystals: Amethyst, aquamarine, blue lace agate, moonstone, opal

Herbs: Ash, birch, watercress, apple, camomile, catnip, gardenia, hawthorn, ivy, myrrh, poppy, rose, violet, willow

Themes: Love, bliss, flow, peace, connection to the heart, mystical, receptive, intuitive, energy of the divine feminine, fluid, transformative, shadow work

Water leads you to the center of your magick, to the effervescent and unyielding core of your power; it guides you back to your heart. What happens in your body when you think of magick? Of love? Of the divine? The beating beast in your chest may growl in awareness at the infinite energy of the cosmos. Or maybe you feel your heart bloom like a tender and beautiful rose awaiting the kiss of the sun, unfurling its petals for the world. Magick is liminal, but we become aware of its effects on us when we pay attention. The way I see it, magick is love and when we actively direct our will and energy to cause change on this realm, it's like being enamored and acting on it. Magick is when you're cradled with so much love that you choose to share it, instead of waiting for someone to show up to give you permission. Sometimes there's heartbreak involved, sometimes there's disappointment, but through it all, magick persists.

To connect with your emotional body and with water means leaning into your intuition and learning what she has to say. It means listening to the messages of the universe and honoring what this feels like in your heart and body. It's time to dive deep into your soul, into the ocean of your subconscious, to willingly shift and embody your desires. You will be uniting with your emotional body and the wonder that lies therein in this chapter through moon magick, shadow work, and sharpening your psychic senses.

My relationship with water:

....

....

....

....

....

How this is a part of my magickal practice:

....

....

....

....

....

My relationship with love and emotions:

....

....

....

....

....

....

....

....

....

....

....

....

....

....

....

....

....

....

....

....

....

Healing Through
Water Rituals

Water's fluidity reminds us of our own; it allows us to be held and supported, to relax and release. Water is the medium in which you can
understand your heart center, excavate your compassion and recog-
nize the language of the mystical and subtle. Through bath rituals and
working with this elemental energy, you can heal while holding space
for yourself. Magickal self-care means ritualizing your self-care
practices—and having plenty of self-compassion. You can turn bathing
and showering into a magickal practice by infusing these mundane ac-
tivities with intention and love.

My relationship with water rituals:

....

....

How I use water to heal:

....

....

....

What I'm looking to enhance with this element:

....

....

....

....

Reflect on an experience you had with water. What was it like? Was it scary, powerful, magickal, exhilarating, or transformative? How would you like to reconnect with this sensation or adopt a different relationship to water?

....

....

....

....

....

....

....

....

....

....

....

....

....

Creating your signature bath recipe

By crafting an intention and using the herbal table of correspondences on page x for guidance, you will formulate your own bath recipes to come back to again and again. Try different combinations, or use these ones as a base, and then record your findings. If you really want to manifest a magickal experience and honor your intention, add incense, crystals, and candles into the mix.

Soak in the tub for at least 15 minutes—the longer the better—as you relax and meditate on your intention with this ritual. Keep in mind you'll need 1 to 2 cups of salt for the bath, and a couple teaspoons of each herb.

My intention: Healing

Salt: Epsom and pink Himalayan

Herbs: Eucalyptus, lavender, spearmint

Oils: Lavender

Crystals: Blue lace agate, amethyst, rose quartz

Additional items: Light blue and white candles

My intention: Love

Salt: Epsom

Herbs: Rose petals, lavender, camomile, honey powder

Oils: Rose, eucalyptus, and lavender

Crystals: Rose quartz

How I felt:

....

....

....

....

....

....

....

What I want to change for next time:

....

....

....

....

....

....

....

My intention: ....

Salt: ....

Herbs: ....

Oils: ....

Crystals: ....

How I felt: ....

What I want to change for next time: ....

My intention: ....

Salt: ....

Herbs: ....

Oils: ....

Crystals: ....

How I felt: ....

What I want to change for next time: ....

My intention: ....

Salt: ....

Herbs: ....

Oils: ....

Crystals: ....

How I felt: ....

What I want to change for next time: ....

Concocting a salt or sugar body scrub

You can use salt or sugar to make a body scrub for the shower. To do this you will need the following:

1 cup fine sea salt or granulated sugar

½ cup liquid coconut oil or olive oil

Herbs of your choice: add 1 teaspoon of each, or more or less depending on the potency you're after

5 to 6 drops of any essential oils

Anything else you want to add, such as lemon juice, honey, or crystals

A jar or container

Jar label or tape

Once you have your intention in mind, gather your ingredients and in a small bowl, mix the salt or sugar and coconut or olive oil, then add the herbs and essential oils, as well as any other ingredients you wish to add. Transfer the mixture into a jar and add a label or piece of tape listing the date and ingredients. Leave it on your altar overnight or under the Full Moon to further charge it, adding any crystals or talismans in, on or near it to boost its magickal properties.

Each time you use the scrub, connect with your intention by saying affirmations, or writing a charm to say to magnify it. If you're manifesting positivity, you can say something like "I release, I release; I release what's no longer serving me" or "I am engulfed in radiance, strength, and positive energy" as you scrub.

My intention: ....

Herbs I used: ....

Essential oils I used: ....

Crystals I worked with: ....

How this made me feel: ....

....

....

Ways I turned this into a ritual: ....

....

....

My intention: ....

Herbs I used: ....

Essential oils I used: ....

Crystals I worked with: ....

How this made me feel: ....

....

....

Ways I turned this into a ritual: ....

....

....

My favorite bath ritual:

....
....
....
....
....
....
....
....
....
....

My favorite shower ritual:

....
....
....
....
....
....
....
....
....
....

Working with the Phases of the Moon

As the ocean is controlled by the wax and wane of the moon, so too are we. We are affected by the way the moon sheds and grows light, and we can work with lunar magick by aligning our cycles with this celestial body. When we coordinate our magick with the moon's gaining and losing light, we practice sympathetic magick, or magick that imitates its desired outcome. Use the pages ahead to track your energy, mood, and magick in accordance with the moon's phases.

● The New Moon

The message: The New Moon is the beginning of the moon's twenty-eight-day cycle and is when we focus on what we want to expand and invoke during the fourteen days preceding the Full Moon. It's a time to go headfirst into our magick and intention-setting, aligning ourselves with our will and what we want to manifest.

The New Moon is for: Shadow work, introspection and goal setting, manifesting, beginning a cycle

How I feel emotionally:

....

....

My energy level on a scale of 1–10:

....

What magick I performed/how I celebrated:

....

....

....

Crystals and herbs I like to work with:

....

....

....

....

Any notes about this phase:

....

....

....

....

....

....

....

....

....

....

....

....

....

....

....

◐The Waxing Moon and First Quarter Moon

The message: The Waxing Moon is the phase between the New Moon and the Full Moon when its light is growing. The First Quarter Moon is halfway between the New Moon and the Full Moon. This is a time to check in with our intentions and the magick we performed during the New Moon to make sure we are still on course, so we can readjust as necessary.

This time is for: Checking in, readjusting, healing, trying new things, manifesting

How I feel emotionally:

....

....

My energy level on a scale of 1–10:

....

What magick I performed/how I celebrated:

....

....

Crystals and herbs I like to work with:

....

....

....

....

Any notes about this phase:

....

....

....

....

....

....

....

....

....

....

....

....

....

....

....

○The Full Moon

The message: The Full Moon is when the light of the sun is reflected on the moon, when the moon is at the height of its power. This is a potent time for practicing all kinds of magick, though banishing is best saved for the Waning or Dark Moon. The Full Moon amplifies our subtle body, intuition, and magick, and is ripe for divination, ritual, and spell work.

The Full Moon is for: Practicing divination, manifesting, healing, blessing a space, sex magick, rituals of love and beauty, tapping into your power, ending a cycle

How I feel emotionally:

....

....

My energy level on a scale of 1–10:

....

What magick I performed/how I celebrated:

....

....

Crystals and herbs I like to work with:

....

....

....

....

Any notes about this phase:

....

....

....

....

....

....

....

....

....

....

....

....

....

....

....

Take a second to study the moon tarot card.

What do you notice?

....

....

....

....

....

....

How does this card make you feel?

....

....

....

....

....

How can you meditate on this to understand the message of the Full Moon more thoroughly?

....

....

....

....

....

◗The Waning Moon and Third Quarter Moon

The message: The Waning Moon is between the Full Moon and the New Moon, when the moon starts to lose light. Remember "wax on, wane off"! The Third Quarter Moon is also halfway between the Full Moon and the New Moon, but when we banish and let go of what we no longer need. It's a great time for protection magick and releasing old patterns and baggage.

This time is for: Banishing, letting go, closing out cycles, addressing what patterns aren't serving you, protecting your energy and spirit and space

How I feel emotionally:

....

....

My energy level on a scale of 1–10:

....

What magick I performed/how I celebrated:

....

....

Crystals and herbs I like to work with:

....

....

....

....

Any notes about this phase:

....

....

....

....

....

....

....

....

....

....

....

....

....

....

....

● The Dark Moon

The message: The Dark Moon happens right before the New Moon, though there's often not a distinction made between the two. This is when the moon reflects no light from the sun, days before the New Moon is exact. This is when we can do our most potent banishing work and shadow work, when we can cleanse our selves and our spaces before the moon starts to wax or gain light.

The Dark Moon is for: Shadow work, banishing, protection, clearing, cleaning your physical and sacred space

How I feel emotionally:

....

....

My energy level on a scale of 1–10:

....

What magick I performed/how I celebrated:

....

....

....

Crystals and herbs I like to work with:

....

....

....

....

Any notes about this phase:

....

....

....

....

....

....

....

....

....

....

....

....

....

....

....

Mantras

We work with mantras to connect to our hearts, remind ourselves of our strength, infuse our intuition with power, and connect to the subtle realm around us. Use these to tap into your inner Priest/ess, into your inner hierophant, into your soul, to remember the magick that is awake and alive within you.

- I honor my shadow as a path to my truest self.

- I follow the path of my intuition and trust its messages.

- I am magickal, mystical, and that witch.

- I am divinely and cosmically guided.

- I embrace the healing journey I'm on with compassion and patience.

- I choose love, I choose peace, I choose healing.

- I am grounded in love.

- I release what's holding me back from my healing.

- I live in alignment with my heart and the energy of divine love.

Now write your own!

- I am .... ,

  .... and ....

- I am ....

- I honor ....

- I embrace .... and ....

- I connect to the element of water through .... ,

  .... and ....

- ....

- ....

- ....

- ....

A Tarot Spread for Gaining Clarity About a Relationship

Our hearts are tender, occasionally fickle creatures. When we are in the throes of love, it can be hard to see clearly and to understand the truth of the matter. We can use the tarot to gain clarity and a new perspective about a relationship, whether it's romantic, platonic, professional, or familial. Use the following spread to tap into your heart with more wisdom and to see a situation from a fresh angle.

Card 1: Where I'm at emotionally

I pulled: ....

My interpretation: ....

....

Card 2: Where the other person is at emotionally

I pulled: ....

My interpretation: ....

....

Card 3: The truth of our relationship

I pulled: ....

My interpretation: ....

....

Card 4: What I'm not seeing

I pulled: ....

My interpretation: ....

....

Card 5: The immediate future

I pulled: ....

My interpretation: ....

....

Card 6: What to do moving forward

I pulled: ....

My interpretation: ....

....

Card 7: The outcome

I pulled: ....

My interpretation: ....

....

Notes or insights about this reading:

....
....
....
....
....
....
....
....
....
....
....
....
....
....
....
....
....
....
....
....
....
....

Rapid-Fire Journal Questions

Answer the following questions to get in touch with water, with your emotional world, your heart, your sensitivity, your magick. Let the answers flow without fear or judgment. You may take a ritual bath or shower first to amplify the elemental power of water.

You are floating in a tranquil sea, supported, cared for, and nurtured. You are at peace. Describe where you are, what you feel, how this feels in your body:

....

....

....

....

....

My intuition is loudest when I:

....

....

This is what my intuition feels like in my body:

....

....

Write a haiku about your heart:

....

....

....

....

....

....

....

Write a poem about the magick of love:

....

....

....

....

....

....

....

....

....

This is how I know I'm psychic:

....

....

....

....

A time when I really felt my intuition was:

....

....

....

....

The clair-sense I feel the most connected to is:

....

....

....

....

Clairvoyance: clear seeing
Clairaudience: clear hearing
Clairsentience: clear feeling
Clairalience: clear smelling
Clairgustance: clear tasting
Claircognizance: clear knowing

Close your eyes and put a hand over your heart. Breathe into this space and ask your heart how it feels, what it needs, and what it wants to tell you. Write or draw your findings below:

Shadow work is when we intentionally integrate and honor the parts of ourselves that we may try to avoid: our shadow. Our shadow is our darkness, the side of ourselves that we reject and have trouble accepting, or that society rejects or deems taboo. We must work with our shadow to be as whole and embodied as possible.

Think of someone who bothers you and annoys you. Write down all of their traits that you dislike and rub you the wrong way:

....

....

....

....

....

....

....

....

....

....

....

....

....

....

Now circle the traits that you have within yourself.

Meditate on these traits as you talk to your shadow. Ask your shadow to take a form, whether it's a monster or what you see in the mirror; remember you are safe and in control and can open your eyes whenever you like.

Write or draw your shadow below:

What did your shadow tell you? How can you work on accepting and integrating these parts of yourself? (Self-love helps!)

....

....

....

....

....

....

....

....

....

....

....

....

....

....

....

....

....

Pick a tarot card to describe your relationship with your shadow and the dark, watery crevices of your heart.

Consider:
What does the card say to you?
What does it mean to you?

Reflect, doodle, write a love letter or poem to your shadow and this card:

SPIRIT:
The Soul

Direction: Up

Archangel: Metatron

Tarot Suit: Major Arcana

Crystals: Herkimer Diamond, labradorite, clear quartz

Themes: The spiritual, enlightenment, connection to source, connection to cosmos, intuition, the subtle body, divine alignment, embodiment of the other elements

Magick illuminates our soul; it transforms us and reminds us of the hermetic and occult truth "as above, so below. As within, so without." As we explore the realms of the mystical, we are led back to this axiom over and over again. The idea that we are reflections of the divine, that we are mirrors to the transcendent experiences of the universe, underlies our ability to use magick to influence change on the physical and astral planes.

Spirit is one of the hardest elements to describe or write about because it's not of this realm. It isn't a physical property like earth, nor is it something we can feel like the wind, or rain, or sunshine. Spirit vibrates within us as we embody the other elements of earth, air, fire, and water. It is the medium through which we work magick, the canvas on which we craft our spells and rituals.

Spirit alchemizes. When we are aligned with our magick, when we are conscious of the energy we are using to shape our reality, and when we use this for the highest good of all involved, we are transmuting and using spirit to grow into a better version of ourselves. Spirit is the connection between the elements, and how we weave our spells.

What was your first experience with magick?

....
....
....

How did it illuminate or inspire you?

....
....
....

Were you the same after this experience?

....
....
....

Calling on the Greek Muses for Inspiration

Born in Pieria, Greece, at the foot of Mount Olympus, the Muses were the patron Goddesses of poets who came to adopt the liberal arts and sciences as their domain. Homer's *Odyssey* lists nine Muses, and according to the poet Hesiod, the Muses were born from the God Zeus, the king of Gods, and Mnemosyne, the Goddess of memory.

Calliope: Muse of epic poetry, with a writing tablet in hand; associated with the God Hermes and the planet Mercury

Clio: Muse of history, seen holding a scroll; associated with the Goddess Selene and the moon

Erato: Muse of lyric and erotic poetry, often playing the lyre; associated with the God Ares and the planet Mars

Euterpe: Muse of music or flutes, often playing the flute; associated with the God Zeus and the planet Jupiter

Melpomene: Muse of tragedy, who holds a tragic mask; associated with the sun

Polyhymnia: Muse of sacred poetry and choral sacred song, with a pensive look on her face; associated with the God Kronos and the planet Saturn

Terpsichore: Muse of dancing and choral singing, shown dancing and holding a lyre; associated with the Goddess Aphrodite and the planet Venus

Thalia: Muse of comedy, depicted holding a comic mask

Urania: Muse of astronomy, represented carrying a globe

The Muse I feel most connected to:

....

If I were a Muse, I would rule over and be associated with:

....

....

Pick one of the Muses and spend some time looking up depictions of her, researching her, noticing what she holds in her hands and what colors she's portrayed in. These are all keys to her magick and clues into how to call upon and channel her.

The Muse I'm working with:

....

....

What I noticed about her:

....

....

....

What she's telling me about her magick:

....

....

....

....

....

....

....

In the *Odyssey*, Homer opens by calling on the Muses. Read it for inspiration, then rewrite it in your own words, in a cadence that suits you. Use the following for guidance in weaving a ritual to invoke the Muses, allowing your creativity and magick to inspire you.

Write an invocation to your chosen Muse. Consider your connection to what she rules over and what is sacred to her and ask how you can invite more of this into your life. Fill in the following and then write your own.

Sacred Muse .... *(their name) of*
.... *(what they rule over), I ask for your inspiration and magick to come to me.*

May you lead me through this path, to the world of expansion and growth so there's no going back. May I learn of your art and soul, and channel this in creations of my own.

May your divine grace help me channel sacred art, for the highest good of all involved.

May this or something better come to me, by your blessing times three.

My invocation:

....

....

....

....

....

....

....

....

....

....

....

....

Dedicate a white candle (to represent a clear mind and clean slate) to the nine Muses or to your chosen muse. Sit with it in meditation and let the Muses know that you want to foster this connection. Ask for their blessing to help you draw down inspiration. Send this intention into the candle, and then dress the candle with any herbs and oils that correspond to your chosen Muse (using the table on page x to help). Light it and let it burn all the way down, or relight it every time you need to channel your Muse. If there's excess wax after burning, you may dispose of it at a three- or four-way intersection, the modern witch's crossroads.

My intention with my Muse or Muses of choice:

....

....

....

....

....

....

How this ritual went:

....

....

....

....

....

....

What other rituals can I craft and sculpt to connect with this Muse?

....

....

....

....

....

....

Mantras

When you work with mantras, you are affirming your magick and power to both yourself and the universe. Work with affirmations to remind yourself of your truth; that you are divine in nature, that your magick knows no bounds, and that you deserve to live the life of your fantasies, and experience as much pure bliss and joy as possible. Use the following affirmations to assert your path, your brilliance, your magick and divinity. Repeat them often.

- I am worthy and deserving of my dreams and desires.

- I am the divine personified.

- I am committed to my magick, to my healing, to my Self.

- I am spirit embodied.

- I am magick.

- I honor my evolution with compassion, patience, and perseverance.

- I am powerful as hell and I am worthy of my desires.

- I embrace my magick.

- I return to my breath and to ritual in moments of fear and uncertainty.

- I am safe, supported, and taken care of by the universe.

- I am healthy, radiant, capable, and mystical as fuck.

Now write your own.

- I am .... ,

  .... and ....

- I am ....

- I honor ....

- I embrace .... and ....

- I connect to the element of spirit through .... ,

  .... and ....

- ....

- ....

- ....

A Tarot Spread to Receive Guidance from the Archangels

Although the archangels appear in Judaism, Christianity, and Islam, these beings of pure light and love also exist outside of these religions, of these boundaries and parameters. The archangels are distillations of the life force of the cosmos; they are messengers and spiritual helpers that we can call on in time of need, or whenever we want their support and guidance. You don't have to believe in a monotheistic religion to work with or believe in them. All you need to do to foster a relationship with the archangels is to invite them in. Since we have free will in this life, the archangels cannot interfere, intervene, or help us out unless we ask. So this tarot spread is not only a way to ask for help but also a channel to receive their messages.

Before you begin, you may ask the archangels for their help, and invite them in so you may connect to and work with their magick. You can even dedicate a candle to them, using instructions on page 63, and light it whenever you want to ask for assistance. Think of a question or query you need some divine guidance with, and then let the tarot and angels illuminate your path. Set up your space, grab your cards, take a few deep, centering breaths, and then ask your questions.

Card 1, Archangel Michael: What is protecting me and guiding me at this time?

I pulled: ....

My interpretation: ....

....

Card 2, Archangel Raphael: What do I need to be gentle with and heal?

I pulled: ....

My interpretation: ....

....

Card 3, Archangel Gabriel: What inspiration can I take from this situation?

I pulled: ....

My interpretation: ....

....

Card 4, Archangel Uriel: What can I do to find grounding and safety?

I pulled: ....

My interpretation: ....

....

Card 5, Archangel Metatron: How am I supported by the universe and cosmos?

I pulled: ....

My interpretation: ....

....

Notes or insights about this reading:

....
....
....
....
....
....
....
....
....
....
....
....
....
....
....
....
....
....
....
....

Working with the Wheel of the Year

One of the ways we can align ourselves with the natural world is by following her seasonal cycles. This is known as the Wheel of the Year to witches, a calendar that marks the passage of time through the solstices, equinoxes, and days in between. When we are conscious of what the celestial bodies are doing, we align with our own magick, too. Keep in mind that the Wheel of the Year is the opposite for the Northern and Southern Hemispheres, and the following dates are for the Northern Hemisphere; arrange your calendar accordingly!

The Equinoxes

The equinoxes mark a point of balance, when day and night are equal length. This is a potent time for magick, as it's an energetic liminal space that also marks the beginning of the season. The exact day of the equinox varies year to year.

The spring equinox, ostara, March 19–21

In Greek mythology, this is when Persephone returns to Earth as the Goddess of Springtime. A celebration of rebirth, warmth, and sensuality, the spring equinox asks us to dwell in pleasure, in the invigorating, and in inspiration. This is the first day of spring, so think of flowers, bunnies, sunshine, fresh air, and new beginnings.

How I celebrate:

....

....

Rituals I perform:

....

....

Crystals I can work with:

....

....

How I decorate my altar:

....

....

The fall equinox, mabon, September 19–21

This is when Persephone is taken by Hades as his consort, assuming her title as Goddess of the Underworld. It's when we reap the rewards of the harvest—physically, spiritually, and emotionally—as we prepare to move deeper into the waning year and its darkness. This is the beginning of fall, so think pumpkins, hot cocoa, warm drinks, colorful leaves, and cozy homes and sacred spaces.

How I celebrate:

....

....

Rituals I perform:

....

....

Crystals I can work with:

....

....

How to decorate my altar:

....

....

The Solstices

The solstices occur when the sun is closest to the earth during its 365-day orbit, and farthest away from the earth. They mark the beginning of a season and either the waxing year—after which the days will get longer and the nights, shorter—or the waning year—after which the nights will get longer and the days, shorter. They're an excellent time to meditate on themes of life, death, and rebirth.

The winter solstice, yule, December 19–21

The winter solstice is the longest night of the year, yet it marks the first day of winter and the beginning of the waxing year, as days get longer and longer after. This is a chance for us to connect with our shadow, to honor what we've experienced, and to remember this is the beginning of a return to light. Think yule logs, the rebirth of the sun, snowflakes, hot cocoa, and spending time with loved ones.

How I celebrate:

....

....

Rituals I perform:

....

....

Crystals I can work with:

....

....

How to decorate my altar:

....

....

The summer solstice, litha, June 19–21

The summer solstice is the first day of summer and the longest day of the year, when the sun is at its strongest and most energized. This is a time to celebrate, to bask in the power of solar energy, and to enjoy all the nostalgia, vibrance, warmth, and prosperity that summer promises. It also marks the beginning of the waning year, since nights get longer and longer after this holiday.

How I celebrate:

....

....

Rituals I perform:

....

....

Crystals I can work with:

....

....

How to decorate my altar:

....

....

The Cross Quarter Days

Cross quarter days fall in between the solstices and equinoxes. They are when the wheel begins to turn, when we feel the shift from one season to another. They mark the middle of a season, and are a time to sit with and honor the energy that emerges before a cyclic shift.

Imbolc, February 1

Imbolc comes in the dead of winter, when we experience a transformation in the frozen tundra around us. This holiday, also known as Candlemass, is sacred to Brigid, the Celtic Goddess of fire and inspiration, and is a return to light, an opportunity for us to focus on the rebirth spring brings that's right around the corner.

How I celebrate:

....

....

....

Rituals I perform:

....

....

....

Crystals I can work with:

....

....

How to decorate my altar:

....

....

Lughnasadh, August 1

The first of three harvest holidays, which include the fall equinox and Samhain, Lughnasadh is when we prepare for the harvest and start thinking about the impending autumn. Named after the Celtic Sun God Lugh, this is a time to bask in and appreciate the energy of the sun and summer.

How I celebrate:

....

....

....

Rituals I perform:

....

....

....

Crystals I can work with:

....

....

How to decorate my altar:

....

....

Beltane, May 1

Also known as May Day, Beltane is a festival of fire and fertility, traditionally celebrated with a Maypole and plenty of bonfires. It is when we can embrace our sexuality, flirt with the divine, and own our inner flame. This is a celebration of spring, and the joy and bliss that the warm months bring.

How I celebrate:

....

....

....

Rituals I perform:

....

....

....

Crystals I can work with:

....

....

How to decorate my altar:

....

....

Samhain, October 31

Perhaps the most beloved holiday of the witch, Samhain is the Witch's New Year, when the veil between the spirit realm and the realm of the living is the thinnest. It is a day to honor our ancestors, reflect on the past year, and set intentions for the year ahead. It is a time to embrace magick and honor our loved ones who have passed by leaving them offerings and dedicating an altar to them.

How I celebrate:

....

....

....

Rituals I perform:

....

....

Crystals I can work with:

....

....

How to decorate my altar:

....

....

Connecting to the Goddess Through Her Aspects of Maiden/Mother/Crone

Archetypes and symbols are the language of the subconscious and offer another medium in which we can commune with the divine. When working with and embodying the divine feminine, think of her threefold nature as the path to embracing her magick. This "Triple Goddess" shines her face through her roles as maiden, mother, and crone.

Hecate, Greek Goddess of the witches, the crossroads, necromancy, and magick, is often portrayed as having three faces that look over the past, the present, and the future. Hecate is often referred to as the Crone Goddess, which is a term we use negatively in pop culture but that holds much meaning and importance in mysticism. By embracing all aspects of the divine feminine as a reflection of our own growth—which may not be linear—we can understand her better and embrace her message with even more empathy, wisdom, and reverence.

The Maiden

In the Maiden aspect, the Goddess is just beginning to embrace her sexuality and sensuality; she is growing into her magick and carving out a name for herself. If you think of the Addams Family, Wednesday embodies this phase. She is excitable and coming into her own, like the maiden Persephone before she is taken to the underworld. This is the Waxing Moon, when the seeds are planted, watered, and germinating—a wonderful energy to work with during new beginnings.

My relationship with this aspect of the Triple Goddess:

....

....

....

....

....

How have I embodied this energy in my own life?

....

....

....

....

....

....

How can I embody this energy moving forward?

....

....

....

....

....

....

Examples of Maiden energy I connect with:

....

....

....

....

....

....

Magick I can work with to ally myself with her:

....

....

....

....

....

....

The Mother

The energy of the Mother is that of the Empress in tarot; she is grounded, and aware of her wisdom and her ebbs and flows. The Mother is a protectress; she has given birth (whether physically, emotionally, or spiritually) to something she is devoted to nurturing. We can see this energy in Morticia from the Addams Family; she cares for her children, and is still committed to her own needs, to her sexuality and magick. We embrace the Mother when we have something or someone we want to protect and nourish and when we want to embody prosperity and abundance.

My relationship with this aspect of the Triple Goddess:

....

....

....

....

....

How have I embodied this energy in my own life?

....

....

....

....

How can I embody this energy moving forward?

....

....

....

....

....

....

Examples of Mother energy I connect with:

....

....

....

....

....

....

Magick I can work with to ally myself with her:

....

....

....

....

....

....

The Crone

Often overlooked and the least represented in pop culture, the Crone is the wisest of the archetypes. She has seen and lived through things we can only imagine, and with that she brings a necessary and grounded perspective. The Crone is filled with wisdom that comes with knowing herself and living in integrity. It's how Grandmama in the Addams Family is respected, revered, and appreciated for her point of view and acumen. This is an archetype and energy of poise, under-standing, and wisdom that only comes with lived experience.

My relationship with this aspect of the Triple Goddess:

....

....

....

....

....

How have I embodied this energy in my own life?

....

....

....

....

....

How can I embody this energy moving forward?

....

....

....

....

....

....

Examples of Crone energy I connect with:

....

....

....

....

....

....

Magick I can work with to ally myself with her:

....

....

....

....

....

....

Creating a Magickal Self-Care Practice

One of the ways we can weave magick into our lives is by integrating it into how we take care of ourselves. We can work with magick to honor the ebbs and flows of our life; we can turn to ritual to find comfort and grounding in the unknown. By considering each piece of the self—physical, mental, emotional, and spiritual—we can nurture practices that support us holistically.

Examples of what this sacred self-care may look like include:

- Journaling about what's making you feel sad or angry or uncomfortable

- Working with the tarot to gain insight and guidance in handling a situation

- Creating a ritual practice that you can come back to when you're feeling ungrounded, anxious, or upset

- Using affirmations for the things you love about yourself and to remind you of your magick

- Gazing at your non-dominant eye in the mirror and voicing out loud what you love about yourself

- Asking for help from a therapist, friend, or family member

- Taking a bath with epsom salt and herbs to soothe your muscles and your soul

- Practicing breath work to release fear or anxiety

- Stomping your feet on the ground to release annoyance or rage and to find more presence in your body

- Writing out what's making you fearful, angry, self-conscious, or embarrassed on a piece of paper and burning it up over a cauldron, fireproof bowl, or pot of water

- Cooking with intention and blessing your food before you consume it.

EARTH, THE PHYSICAL BODY

Magick and rituals I work with to take care of myself:

- ○ Grounding

- ○ EFT tapping

- ○ Yoga

My practices:

....

....

AIR, THE MENTAL BODY

Magick and rituals I work with to take care of myself:

- ○ Journaling

- ○ Breath work

- ○ Writing a gratitude list

My practices:

....

....

WATER, THE EMOTIONAL BODY

Magick and rituals I work with to take care of myself:

- ○ Taking a ritual bath

- ○ Blessing myself with holy water

- ○ Crying

My practices:

....

....

FIRE, THE SPIRITUAL BODY

Magick and rituals I work with to take care of myself:

- ○ Burning a letter

- ○ Practicing candle magick

- ○ Working with sexual energy and sex magick

My practices:

....

....

SPIRIT, THE SOUL

Magick and rituals I work with to take care of myself:

- ○ Pulling tarot cards

- ○ Working with the Divine Feminine through meditation

- ○ Erecting and dedicating an altar

My practices:

....

....

Notes on how to adopt practices that serve my spiritual, emotional, mental, and physical body:

....

....

....

....

....

....

....

....

....

....

....

....

....

....

....

....

....

....

....

Meditation and Visualization Practice: Working with Colors and Light

We can fine-tune our intuition and strengthen our aura by meditating with colors and light. This is easy, effective, and fun; you can meditate with any color that calls to you, and I encourage you to experiment with colors and techniques. The premise is simple: get into a comfortable position, then come back to the present and your breath, and find a sense of center. Visualize a ball of light above your head, glowing in a color of your choice. Breathe this light down into your body, growing brighter until it's radiating through you and around you. Feel the light enveloping you for as long as you wish, and then as you're ready, open your eyes.

RED

Energy: Strong, rooted in the physical, forceful, confident

Associated chakra: Root

My experience visualizing with red:

Crystals, animals, tarot cards, clothing, people, or things that connect me to this color's energy:

....

LIGHT PINK

Energy: Soft, romantic, loving, empathic, sensitive, heart opening
My experience visualizing with light pink:

....

Crystals, animals, tarot cards, clothing, people, or things that connect me to this color's energy:

....

MAGENTA

Energy: Energizing, sultry, flirty, vibrant, loving, grounded in the energy of the heart
My experience visualizing with magenta:

....

Crystals, animals, tarot cards, clothing, people, or things that connect me to this color's energy:

....

ORANGE

Energy: Energizing, warm, vibrant, expressive, creative, confident
Associated chakra: Sacral

My experience visualizing with orange:

....

Crystals, animals, tarot cards, clothing, people, or things that connect
me to this color's energy:

....

YELLOW

Energy: Revitalizing, warm, powerful, sunny, inspiring, optimistic,
creative, rich, abundant
Associated chakra: Solar plexus
My experience visualizing with yellow:

....

Crystals, animals, tarot cards, clothing, people, or things that connect
me to this color's energy:

....

GOLD

Energy: Healing, protective, energizing, solar power, abundant,
inspiring
My experience visualizing with gold:

....

Crystals, animals, tarot cards, clothing, people, or things that connect
me to this color's energy:

....

GREEN

Energy: Lucky, abundant, heart opening, grounding, supportive, money magick, loving, soothing

Associated chakra: Heart

My experience visualizing with green:

....

Crystals, animals, tarot cards, clothing, people, or things that connect me to this color's energy:

....

BLUE

Energy: Calming, relaxing, tranquil, healing, supportive, soothing, centering

Associated chakra: Throat

My experience visualizing with blue:

....

Crystals, animals, tarot cards, clothing, people, or things that connect me to this color's energy:

....

INDIGO

Energy: Intuitive, psychic, mystical, calming, healing, relaxing

Associated chakra: Third eye

My experience visualizing with indigo:

....

Crystals, animals, tarot cards, clothing, people, or things that connect me to this color's energy:

....

VIOLET

Energy: Psychic, mystical, sensual, high priestess, royal, expansive
Associated chakra: Crown and Third eye
My experience visualizing with violet:

....

Crystals, animals, tarot cards, clothing, people, or things that connect me to this color's energy:

....

WHITE

Energy: Healing, clearing, divine, cleansing, protective, supportive, the pure light of the universe, divine
Associated chakra: Crown
My experience visualizing with white:

....

Crystals, animals, tarot cards, clothing, people, or things that connect me to this color's energy:

....

Rapid-Fire Journal Questions

Answer these questions to get in touch with spirit, with your divine essence, with magick, with ritual, with the self. Channel your higher self; pull some tarot cards; make tea or grab a glass of water; and answer them without shame, with honesty, integrity, and compassion.

We can understand the universal wisdom of spirit through storytelling and mythology. Through myth, eternal truths are captured and shared, framed through drama and theater so we can learn their messages. We can work with this same concept to craft our own mythology.

If I was a God or Goddess, what would I rule over?

....

....

What would my origin story be?

....

....

....

What hardships in life have I gone through that remind me of my
resilience and add to this mythos?

....

....

What would my ritual attire be? How would I be dressed?

....

....

How would I be immortalized?

....

....

What would my temple or sacred space look like?

....

....

How is this decorated?

....

....

Where is it located?

....

....

What does it smell like, sound like, feel like?

....

....

What offerings would devotees bring to me?

....

....

What is my most memorable and impactful experience with magick? Close your eyes and feel it.

....

....

How old was I?

....

....

What happened? Did it profoundly alter or impact my life?

....

....

What does magick feel like to me now?

....

....

How has this changed, transformed, and evolved since my first experience?

....

....

....

What rituals and spells and practices can I return to in order to reconnect with the magickal and mystical within myself?

....

....

What element am I most attuned to?

....

....

What element is the most elusive, the most difficult for me to connect with?

....

....

....

What sort of rituals can I create to find balance with this element, and to invite more into my life?

....

....

....

What's my favorite ritual to work with to connect with earth?

....
....
....

Air?

....
....
....

Fire?

....
....
....

Water?

....
....
....

Spirit?

....
....
....

Pick a tarot card that resonates with you right now.

What does it say to me?

....

....

How can I embody its energy?

....

....

....

Through glamour?

....

....

....

Through ritual?

....

....

....

Through art or poetry?

....

....

....

Describe the card to someone who's not familiar with it.

....

....

Who are my guardian angels?

....

....

My spirit guides?

....

....

What souls lead me toward magick, imagination, and wonder? They can be living or deceased, such as an ancestor; a beloved friend; an artist; or a celebrity or an icon who serves as your muse. What offerings can I leave this person?

....

....

....

What inspiration or support or magick do they share with me?

....

....

....

ACKNOWLEDGMENTS

I want to thank the Goddess and the divine, for allowing me to share my heart and magick. I also want to thank my wonderful team at TarcherPerigee, my editor, Nina Shield; Roshe Anderson; and Katie MacLeod, and my literary agent, Jill Marr. I want to thank my family, my amazing parents, my twin and Zanya, my grandma Tita, and all the friends and coven who have been integral in my growth and in my work. And I want to thank all the witches, mystics, occultists, and wise men and women who have supported me and led me on this path, both in the physical and in the spirit realm.

ABOUT THE AUTHOR

Gabriela Herstik is a fashion alchemist, writer, and witch living in Los Angeles. She is the author of *Bewitching the Elements: A Guide to Empowering Yourself Through Earth, Air, Fire, Water, and Spirit* and *Inner Witch: A Modern Guide to the Ancient Craft*. She has written for publications such as *Vogue International, NYLON, Allure, Dazed Beauty, Glamour,* and more and is the author of the "High Priestess" column on *High Times Magazine.* Gabriela has been a practicing witch for more than thirteen years and is a devotee and Priestess of the Goddess of Love. She believes magick is for everyone.